DOUBLE DELIGHT

Colour and Shape

Mary Novick & Sybel Harlin

SOUTHWOOD
B O O K S

white circles

Marzipan Roses

To decorate a cake, shape
the roses in a variety of
colours and sizes then
arrange on top.

1 Form a small ball of coloured marzipan into a cone shape.
This forms the central core which supports the petals.

2 Take a piece of marzipan about the size of a large pea, and
make a petal shape that is thicker at the base.

3 Wrap the petal around the cone, pressing the petal to the
cone to secure. Bend back the ends of the petal to curl. Repeat
with more petals, each overlapping. Make some petals bigger
until the required size is achieved.

Marzipan

Marzipan can be used on its
own, under an icing or for
modelling decorations.

Makes 450g/1lb/3 cups
225g/8oz/2 cups ground almonds
*115g/4oz/generous ½ cup caster
  (superfine) sugar*
*115g/4oz/1 cup icing
  (confectioners') sugar, sifted*
5ml/1 tsp lemon juice
a few drops of almond extract
1 egg or 1 egg white

1 Stir the ground almonds and sugars together in a bowl until
evenly mixed. Make a well in the centre and add the lemon
juice, almond extract and enough egg or egg white to mix to a
soft but firm dough, using a wooden spoon.

2 Form the marzipan into a ball. Lightly dust a surface with icing
sugar and knead the marzipan until smooth. Wrap in clear film
(plastic wrap) or store in a plastic bag until needed. Tint with
food colouring if required.

Sugarpaste Icing

Sugarpaste icing is
wonderfully pliable and can
be coloured, moulded and
shaped in imaginative ways.

Makes 350g/12oz/2¼ cups
1 egg white
15ml/1 tbsp liquid glucose, warmed
*350g/12oz/3 cups icing
  (confectioners') sugar, sifted*

1 Put the egg white and glucose in a mixing bowl. Stir them
together to break up the egg white.

2 Add the icing sugar and mix together with a metal spatula,
using a chopping action, until well blended and the icing begins
to bind together.

3 Knead the mixture with your fingers until it forms a ball.

4 Knead the sugarpaste on a work surface that has been lightly
dusted with icing sugar for several minutes until it is smooth,
soft and pliable.

5 If the icing is too soft, knead in some more sifted sugar until it
reaches the right consistency.

Cook's Tips
• *Sugarpaste icing is sometimes known as rolled fondant and
is available ready made in sugarcraft stores. It is easy to make
yourself but if you are using a large quantity and are in a hurry
you could purchase it ready made. It is available in a variety
of colours.*
• *If you want to make the sugarpaste in advance wrap it
up tightly in a plastic bag. The icing will keep for about
three weeks.*
• *The paste is easy to colour with paste colours; add a little at
a time using the tip of a knife.*
• *Roll out sugarpaste on a surface lightly sprinkled with icing
(confectioners') sugar or a little white vegetable fat (shortening)
to avoid the paste sticking.*

Energy 2357kcal/9874kJ; Fat 131.1g, Saturated fat 11.5g; Carbohydrate 255.9g; Fibre 16.6g

Energy 1435kcal/6123kJ; Fat 0g, Saturated fat 0g; Carbohydrate 377.6g; Fibre 0g

Royal Icing

Royal icing gives a professional finish. This recipe makes enough icing to cover the top and sides of an 18cm/7in cake.

Makes 675g/1½lb/4½ cups
3 egg whites
about 675g/1½lb/6 cups
*   icing (confectioners')*
*   sugar, sifted*
7.5ml/1½ tsp glycerine
a few drops of lemon juice
food colouring (optional)

1 Put the egg whites in a bowl and stir lightly with a fork to break them up.

2 Add the sifted icing sugar gradually, beating well with a wooden spoon after each addition.

3 Add enough icing sugar to make a smooth, shiny icing that has the consistency of very stiff meringue.

4 Beat in the glycerine, lemon juice and food colouring, if using.

5 Leave for 1 hour before using, covered with damp clear film (plastic wrap), then stir to burst any air bubbles.

Cook's Tips
• The icing will keep for up to three days in a refrigerator, stored in a plastic container with a tight-fitting lid.
• This recipe is for an "icing" consistency suitable for flat-icing a marzipanned rich fruit cake. When the spoon is lifted, the icing should form a sharp point, with a slight curve at the end, known as "soft peak". For piping, the icing needs to be slightly stiffer. It should form a fine sharp peak when the spoon is lifted.
• Royal icing is not appropriate for a sponge cake, as its stiff consistency would easily drag on the surface.
• Never use royal icing direct on to the cake's surface; a layer of marzipan will make a smooth surface for icing and stop cake crumbs mixing with the icing.

Butter Icing

The creamy rich flavour and silky smoothness of butter icing is popular with both children and adults.

Makes 350g/12oz/1½ cups
75g/3oz/6 tbsp soft margarine or
*   butter, softened*
225g/8oz/2 cups icing
*   (confectioners') sugar, sifted*
5ml/1 tsp vanilla extract
10–15ml/2–3 tsp milk

For the flavourings
Chocolate: blend 15ml/1 tbsp
*   unsweetened cocoa powder with*
*   15ml/1 tbsp hot water. Cool*
*   before beating into the icing.*

Coffee: blend 10ml/2 tsp coffee
*   powder with 15ml/1 tbsp*
*   boiling water. Omit the milk.*
*   Cool before beating the mixture*
*   into the icing.*

Lemon, orange or lime: substitute
*   the vanilla extract and milk*
*   with lemon, orange or lime juice*
*   and 10ml/2 tsp of finely grated*
*   citrus rind. Omit the rind if*
*   using the icing for piping.*
*   Lightly tint the icing with food*
*   colouring, if you like.*

1 Put the margarine or butter, icing sugar, vanilla extract and 5ml/1 tsp of the milk in a bowl.

2 Beat with a wooden spoon or an electric mixer, adding sufficient extra milk to give a light, smooth and fluffy consistency. For flavoured butter icing, follow the instructions above for the flavour of your choice.

Cook's Tips
• The icing will keep for up to three days in an airtight container stored in a refrigerator.
• Butter icing can be coloured with paste colours. Add a little at a time using a cocktail stick (toothpick) until you reach the desired shade.
• You can apply butter icing with a knife and make a smooth finish, or you can pipe the icing on to your cake using a plain or fluted nozzle, or use a serrated scraper for a ridged finish.

Energy 2694kcal/11494kJ; Fat 0g, Saturated fat 0g; Carbohydrate 705.4g; Fibre 0g

Energy 1461kcal/6149kJ; Fat 62g, Saturated fat 0.5g; Carbohydrate 238g; Fibre 0g

Fudge Frosting

A darkly delicious frosting, this can transform a simple sponge cake into one worthy of a very special occasion.

Makes 350g/12oz/1½ cups
50g/2oz plain
  (semisweet) chocolate
225g/8oz icing (confectioners')
  sugar, sifted
50g/2oz/4 tbsp butter
45ml/3 tbsp milk or single
  (light) cream
5ml/1 tsp vanilla extract

1 Break or chop the chocolate into small pieces. Put the chocolate, icing sugar, butter, milk or cream and vanilla extract in a heavy pan.

2 Stir over a very low heat until both the chocolate and the butter have melted. Remove the mixture from the heat and stir until it is evenly blended.

3 Beat the icing frequently as it cools until it thickens sufficiently to use for spreading or piping.

4 Use the icing immediately and work as quickly as possible once it has reached the right consistency. If you let it cool too much it will become too thick to work with.

Cook's Tips
• Spread fudge frosting smoothly over the cake or swirl it. Or be even more elaborate with a little piping – it really is very versatile.
• This recipe makes enough to fill and coat the top and sides of a 20cm/8in or 23cm/9in round sponge cake.
• This icing should be used immediately.
• Use a good quality chocolate so that you achieve a pronounced flavour for this frosting.
• As the frosting contains cream it is best to keep the finished cake in the refrigerator until ready to serve.

Energy 1534kcal/6468kJ; Fat 55.9g, Saturated fat 34.9g; Carbohydrate 269.3g; Fibre 1.3g

Crème au Beurre

The rich, smooth texture of this icing makes it ideal for spreading, filling or piping on to cakes and gateaux.

Makes 350g/12oz/1½ cups
60ml/4 tbsp water
75g/3oz/6 tbsp caster
  (superfine) sugar
2 egg yolks
150g/5oz/10 tbsp unsalted
  (sweet) butter, softened

For the flavourings
Citrus: replace water with orange, lemon or lime juice and 10ml/ 2 tsp grated rind
Chocolate: add 50g/2oz plain (semisweet) chocolate, melted
Coffee: add 10ml/2 tsp instant coffee granules, dissolved in 5ml/1 tsp boiling water, cooled

1 Put the water in a pan and bring to the boil, then stir in the sugar. Heat gently, stirring, until the sugar has dissolved.

2 Boil rapidly until the mixture becomes syrupy, or reaches the "thread" stage (107°C/225°F on a sugar thermometer). To test, place a little syrup on the back of a dry teaspoon. Press a second teaspoon on to the syrup and gently pull apart. The syrup should form a fine thread. If not, return to the heat, boil rapidly and re-test a minute later.

3 Whisk the egg yolks together in a bowl. Continue to whisk while slowly adding the sugar syrup in a thin stream. Whisk until thick, pale and cool. Beat the butter until light and fluffy. Add the egg mixture gradually, beating well after each addition, until thick and fluffy.

4 For Chocolate or Coffee Crème au Beurre, fold in the flavouring at the end.

Cook's Tip
It is important that the syrup reaches the correct stage and does not cook any further, as it will become too firm and you will not be able to whisk it into the egg yolks smoothly.

Energy 1534kcal/6354kJ; Fat 134.3g, Saturated fat 81.3g; Carbohydrate 79.3g; Fibre 0g

American Frosting

A light marshmallow icing which crisps on the outside when left to dry, this versatile frosting may be swirled or peaked into a soft coating.

Makes 350g/12oz/1½ cups
1 egg white
30ml/2 tbsp water
15ml/1 tbsp golden (light corn) syrup
5ml/1 tsp cream of tartar
175g/6oz/1½ cups icing (confectioners') sugar, sifted

1 Place the egg white with the water, golden syrup and cream of tartar in a heatproof bowl. Whisk together until blended.

2 Stir the icing sugar into the mixture and place the bowl over a pan of simmering water. Whisk until the mixture becomes thick and white.

3 Remove the bowl from the pan and continue to whisk the frosting until cool and thick, and the mixture stands up in soft peaks. Use immediately to fill or cover cakes.

Caramel Icing

A rich-tasting icing that makes a lovely cake topping.

Makes 450g/1lb/2 cups
75ml/5 tbsp creamy milk

75g/3oz/6 tbsp butter
30 ml/2 tbsp caster (superfine) sugar
350g/12oz/3 cups icing (confectioners') sugar

1 Warm the milk and butter in a pan. Heat the caster sugar in another pan over medium heat until it turns golden. Immediately remove from the heat before the caramel darkens.

2 Pour the milk mixture over the caramel and return the pan to a low heat. Heat the mixture until the caramel has dissolved, stirring occasionally. Sift in the icing sugar a little at a time, and beat with a wooden spoon until the icing is smooth. Use immediately.

Glacé Icing

An instant icing for quickly finishing the tops of large or small cakes.

Makes 350g/12oz/1½ cup
225g/8oz/2 cups icing (confectioners') sugar
30–45ml/2–3 tbsp hot water
food colouring (optional)

For the flavourings
Citrus: replace the water with orange, lemon or lime juice
Chocolate: sift 10ml/2 tsp unsweetened cocoa powder with the icing (confectioners') sugar
Coffee: replace the water with strong, liquid coffee

1 Sift the icing sugar into a bowl. Using a wooden spoon, gradually stir in enough of the hot water to obtain the consistency of thick cream.

2 Beat until white and smooth, and the icing thickly coats the back of the spoon. Tint with a few drops of food colouring, if you wish, or flavour the icing as suggested above. Use immediately to cover the top of the cake.

Simple Piped Flowers

Bouquets of iced blooms, such as roses, pansies and bright summer flowers, make colourful cake decorations.

Makes 350g/12oz/1½ cup
225g/8oz/2 cups icing (confectioners') sugar
30–45ml/2–3 tbsp hot water

1 For a rose, make a fairly firm icing. Colour the icing. Fit a petal nozzle into a paper piping (icing) bag, half-fill with icing and fold over the top to seal. Hold the piping bag so that the wider end is pointing at what will be the base of the rose and hold a cocktail stick (toothpick) in the other hand.

2 Pipe a small cone shape around the tip of the stick, pipe a petal halfway around the cone, lifting it so that it is at an angle and curling outwards, turning the stick at the same time. Repeat with more overlapping petals. Remove from the stick and leave to dry.

Top: Energy 746kcal/3181kJ; Fat 0g, Saturated fat 0g; Carbohydrate 194.7g; Fibre 0g
Above: Energy 2070kcal/8850kJ; Fat 604g, Saturated fat 38.2g; Carbohydrate 404.5g; Fibre 0g

Top: Energy 887kcal/3782kJ; Fat 0g, Saturated fat 0g; Carbohydrate 235.1g; Fibre 0g
Above: Energy 887kcal/3782kJ; Fat 0g, Saturated fat 0g; Carbohydrate 235.1g; Fibre 0g

Honey Icing

A simple and tasty topping for cakes.

Makes 275g/10oz/1¼ cups
75g/3oz/6 tbsp butter, softened

175g/6oz/1½ cups icing (confectioners') sugar
15ml/1 tbsp clear honey
15ml/1 tbsp lemon juice

1 Put the softened butter into a bowl and gradually sift over the icing sugar, beating well after each addition.

2 Beat in the honey and lemon juice and combine well. Spread over the cake immediately.

Butterscotch Frosting

Soft light brown sugar and treacle make a rich and tempting frosting for cakes.

Makes 675g/1½lb/3 cups
75g/3oz/6 tbsp unsalted (sweet) butter
45ml/3 tbsp milk
25g/1oz/2 tbsp soft light brown sugar
15ml/1 tbsp black treacle (molasses)
350g/12oz/3 cups icing (confectioners') sugar, sifted

For the flavourings
Citrus: replace the treacle with golden (light corn) syrup and add 10ml/2 tsp finely grated orange, lemon or lime rind
Chocolate: sift 15ml/1 tbsp unsweetened cocoa powder with the icing (confectioners') sugar
Coffee: replace the treacle (molasses) with 15ml/1 tbsp coffee granules

1 Place the butter, milk, sugar and treacle in a bowl over a pan of simmering water. Stir until the butter melts and the sugar dissolves completely.

2 Remove from the heat and stir in the icing sugar. Beat until smooth. For different flavourings, follow the instructions above. Pour over the cake, or cool for a thicker consistency.

Chocolate Fudge Icing

A rich glossy icing which sets like chocolate fudge, this is versatile enough to smoothly coat, swirl or pipe, depending on the temperature of the icing when it is used.

Makes 450g/1lb/2 cups
115g/4oz plain (semisweet) chocolate, in squares
50g/2oz/¼ cup unsalted (sweet) butter
1 egg, beaten
175g/6oz/1½ cups icing (confectioners') sugar, sifted

1 Place the chocolate and butter in a heatproof bowl over a pan of hot water.

2 Stir the mixture occasionally with a wooden spoon until both the chocolate and butter are melted. Add the egg and beat well until thoroughly combined.

3 Remove the bowl from the pan and stir in the icing sugar, then beat until smooth and glossy.

4 Pour immediately over the cake for a smooth finish, or leave to cool for a thicker spreading or piping consistency.

Chocolate Curls

These tasty curls look spectacular on a gateau.

Makes around 20 curls
115g/4 oz plain (semisweet) chocolate

1 Melt the chocolate, then pour on to a smooth surface, such as marble or plastic laminate. Spread evenly over the surface with a palette knife. Leave to cool slightly.

2 Hold a large, sharp knife at a 45° angle to the chocolate and push it along the chocolate in short sawing movements from right to left to make curls. Lift off with the knife and leave to cool.

Top: Energy 1291kcal/5420kJ; Fat 61.6g; Saturated fat 39.1g; Carbohydrate 194.8g; Fibre 0g
Above: Energy 2095kcal/8850kJ; Fat 62.4g; Saturated fat 39.5g; Carbohydrate 404.5g; Fibre 0g

Top: Energy 1722kcal/7235kJ; Fat 78.8g, Saturated fat 46.9g; Carbohydrate 256.2g; Fibre 2.9g
Above: Energy 29kcal/123kJ; Fat 1.6g; Saturated fat 1g; Carbohydrate 3.7g; Fibre 0.1g

Apricot Glaze

It is a good idea to make a large quantity of apricot glaze, especially when making celebration cakes.

Makes 450g/1lb/1½ cups
450g/1lb/generous 1½ cups apricot jam
45ml/3 tbsp water

1 Place the jam and water in a pan. Heat gently, stirring occasionally, until the jam has melted.

2 Boil the jam rapidly for 1 minute, then rub through a sieve, pressing the fruit against the sides of the sieve with the back of a wooden spoon.

3 Discard the skins left in the sieve.

4 Use the warmed glaze to brush cakes before applying marzipan, or use for glazing fruits on gateaux and cakes.

Pastillage

This paste sets very hard and is used for making firm decorative structures from icing sugar.

Makes 350g/12oz/1¼ cups
300g/11oz icing (confectioners') sugar
1 egg white
10ml/2 tsp gum tragacanth

1 In a large bowl, sift most of the icing sugar over the egg white, a little at a time, stirring continuously until the mixture sticks together.

2 Add the gum tragacanth and transfer the mixture to a work surface which has been dusted with icing sugar.

3 Knead the mixture well until the ingredients are thoroughly combined and the paste has a smooth texture.

4 Knead in the remaining icing sugar and mix until stiff.

Sugar-frosting Flowers

Choose edible flowers such as pansies, primroses, violets, roses, freesias, apple blossom, wild bergamot (monarda), borage, carnations, honeysuckle, jasmine and pot marigolds.

Makes 10–15 flowers, depending on their size
1 egg white
caster (superfine) sugar
10–15 edible flowers

1 Lightly beat an egg white in a small bowl and sprinkle some caster (superfine) sugar on a plate.

2 Wash the flowers then dry on kitchen paper. Evenly brush both sides of the petals with the egg white. Hold the flower by its stem over a plate lined with kitchen paper, sprinkle it evenly with the sugar, then shake off any excess. Place on a wire rack covered with kitchen paper and leave to dry in a warm place.

Glossy Chocolate Icing

A rich smooth glossy icing, this can be made with plain or milk chocolate.

Makes 350g/12oz/1¼ cups
175g/6oz plain (semisweet) chocolate
150ml/¼ pint/⅔ cup single (light) cream

1 Break up the chocolate into small pieces and place it in a pan with the cream.

2 Heat gently, stirring occasionally, until the chocolate has melted and the mixture is smooth.

3 Allow the icing to cool until it is thick enough to coat the back of a wooden spoon. Use it at this stage for a smooth glossy icing, or allow it to thicken to obtain an icing which can be swirled or patterned with a cake decorating scraper.

Top: Energy 1175kcal/5022kJ; Fat 0g, Saturated fat 0g; Carbohydrate 311.9g; Fibre 0g
Above: Energy 1453kcal/6190kJ; Fat 5.5g; Saturated fat 1.6g; Carbohydrate 365.8g; Fibre 0g

Top: Energy 6kcal/24kJ; Fat 0g; Saturated fat 0g; Carbohydrate 1.1g; Fibre 0.1g
Above: Energy 1182kcal/4937kJ; Fat 77.7g, Saturated fat 47.6g; Carbohydrate 114.4g; Fibre 4.4g

Petal Paste

Makes 500g/1¼lb

10ml/2 tsp powdered gelatine
25ml/1½ tbsp cold water
10ml/2 tsp liquid glucose
10ml/2 tsp white vegetable
   fat (shortening)

450g/1lb/4 cups icing
   (confectioners') sugar, sifted
5ml/1 tsp gum tragacanth
1 egg white

1 Place the gelatine, water, liquid glucose and white fat in a heatproof bowl set over a pan of hot water until melted, stirring occasionally.

2 Remove the bowl from the heat.

3 Sift the icing sugar and gum tragacanth into a large bowl. Make a well in the centre and add the egg white and the gelatine mixture.

4 Thoroughly combine the ingredients to form a soft malleable white paste.

5 Knead the paste on a surface dusted with icing sugar until smooth, white and free from cracks.

6 Place in a plastic bag or wrap in clear film (plastic wrap), sealing well to exclude all the air.

7 Leave the paste for about two hours before using, then knead again and use small pieces at a time, leaving the remaining petal paste well sealed.

Piping Twisted Ropes

Fit nozzles nos 43 or 44, or a writing nozzle, into a baking parchment piping (icing) bag and half-fill with royal icing. Hold the bag at a slight angle and pipe in a continuous line with even pressure, twisting the bag as you pipe.

Energy 1888kcal/8044kJ; Fat 8.2g, Saturated fat 3.6g; Carbohydrate 478.3g; Fibre 0g

Marbling

Sugarpaste lends itself to tinting in all shades and marbling is a good way to colour the paste.

1 Using a cocktail stick (toothpick), add a little of the chosen edible food colour to some sugarpaste icing. Do not knead the food colouring fully into the icing.

2 When the sugarpaste is rolled out, the colour is dispersed in such a way that it gives a marbled appearance.

Meringue Frosting

This wonderfully light and delicate frosting needs to be used immediately.

Makes 450g/1lb/1½ cups

2 egg whites
115g/4oz/1 cup icing
   (confectioners') sugar, sifted
150g/5oz/⅔ cup unsalted
   (sweet) butter, softened

For the flavourings
Citrus: 10ml/2 tsp finely grated
   orange, lemon or lime rind.
Chocolate: 50g/2oz plain
   (semisweet) chocolate, melted
Coffee: 10ml/2 tsp coffee
   granules, blended with 5ml/
   1 tsp boiling water, cooled

1 Whisk the egg whites in a clean, heatproof bowl, add the icing sugar and gently whisk to mix well. Place the bowl over a pan of simmering water and whisk until thick and white. Remove the bowl from the pan and continue to whisk until cool when the meringue stands up in soft peaks.

2 Beat the butter in a separate bowl until light and fluffy. Add the meringue gradually, beating well after each addition, until thick and fluffy. Fold in the chosen flavouring, using a metal spatula, until evenly blended. Use immediately for coating, filling and piping on to cakes.

Energy 1592kcal/6620kJ; Fat 123.3g, Saturated fat 78.1g; Carbohydrate 121.1g; Fibre 0g